CROCHETING
FOR FUN!

by Lisa Bullard

Content Adviser: Randy Cavaliere, Certified Crochet Teacher, Craft Yarn Council of America, Brooklyn, New York
Reading Adviser: Frances J. Bonacci, Ed.D., Reading Specialist, Cambridge, Massachusetts

Compass Point Books ✦ Minneapolis, Minnesota

Compass Point Books
151 Good Counsel Drive
P.O. Box 669
Mankato, MN 56002-0669

 This book was manufactured with paper containing at least 10 percent post-consumer waste.

Photographs ©: David Crowther/iStockphoto, cover (left), 43 (right); Heidi Priesnitz/iStockphoto, cover (right, burgundy); Dennis Tokarzewski/Shutterstock, cover (right, purple), 20; Hannu Liivaar/Shutterstock, cover (right, green), back cover; AP Images/*Eau Claire Leader-Telegram*, Shane Opatz, 4–5; Kevin Jeffrey, 5 (back), 7 (right), 14–15, 17 (bottom), 22–23 (top), 26, 27, 28–29, 38 (all), 39; Library of Congress, 6–7; Karon Dubke/Capstone Press, 8, 11 (top), 16–17, 18 (all), 19, 21, 22–23 (bottom), 30–31, 32–33; Miles Boyer/Shutterstock, 9, 47; Teresa Levite/123RF, 10; Christophe Testi/Shutterstock, 11 (middle); David Brimm/Shutterstock, 11 (bottom); Nancy Catherine Walker/iStockphoto, 16 (bottom); Alina Solovyova-Vincent/iStockphoto, 24 (bottom); Loretta Hostettler/iStockphoto, 24–25; Frederick Lewis/Lambert/ Getty Images, 34 (bottom); Nancy Nehring/iStockphoto, 34–35; AP Images/Cobus Bodenstein, 36; Jou Ling Yee/Amigurumi Kingdom, 37; AP Images/Julie Jacobson, 40; AP Images/Stephan Savoia, 41; The Granger Collection, New York, 42 (all), 45; AP Images/Keystone, Laurent Gillieron, 43 (left); AP Images/Fabian Bimmer, 44 (top); AP Images/Ross D. Franklin, 44 (bottom).

Acknowledgment: Special thanks to Kevin Jeffrey, Julie Gassman, Stephanie Goerger Sandahl, and Kallan LeAnn Sandahl for their help with and enthusiasm for this book.

Editor: Brenda Haugen
Page Production: The Design Lab
Photo Researcher: Eric Gohl
Illustrator: Ashlee Suker
Art Director: LuAnn Ascheman-Adams
Creative Director: Keith Griffin
Editorial Director: Nick Healy
Managing Editor: Catherine Neitge

Library of Congress Cataloging-in-Publication Data
Bullard, Lisa.
  Crocheting for fun! / by Lisa Bullard.
    p. cm. — (For fun)
  Includes index.
  ISBN 978-0-7565-3861-3 (library binding)
  1. Crocheting—Juvenile literature. I. Title. II. Series.
  TT820.B934 2008
  746.43'4—dc22   2008008272

Visit Compass Point Books on the Internet at *www.compasspointbooks.com*
or e-mail your request to *custserv@compasspointbooks.com*

Table of Contents

Note: In this book, there are two kinds of vocabulary words. Crocheting Words to Know are words specific to crocheting. They are defined on page 46. Other Words to Know are helpful words that are not related only to crocheting. They are defined on page 47.

In the Loop

Would you like to make clothes, gifts, and eye-catching items for your home? When you learn to crochet, you can make projects that show your style.

Knitting—crochet's popular cousin—requires two or more needles. However, you need only one simple tool to crochet: the crochet hook. It is used to connect loops of yarn or other materials.

Experts believe crochet is a new craft compared to other fiber arts such as weaving. However, it has still been an important part of history and has grown to be a popular craft around the world. Learn to crochet, and join the millions of people who are proud to show off their latest "I-made-it-myself" creations!

Say What?

The word crochet (pronounced *crow-SHAY*) comes from the French word for "hook."

Handcraft With a Past

Was crocheting first done in China or South America? There are many theories, but nobody knows for sure. What experts do know is that two types of crochet were found in Europe in the 1800s. The first type often used thin white cotton thread. This thread was used to crochet beautiful items that often were used as decorations. The second type of crochet is sometimes called shepherd's knitting. This simple crochet stitch was used to make warm woolen mittens and caps in colder regions.

Crochet's popularity has seen many ups and downs. During the late 1960s and early 1970s, crocheted clothing was considered "cool," but then it lost popularity. Today crochet is a fast-growing craft again. Millions of people crochet for fun, and crocheted clothing often appears on fashion runways.

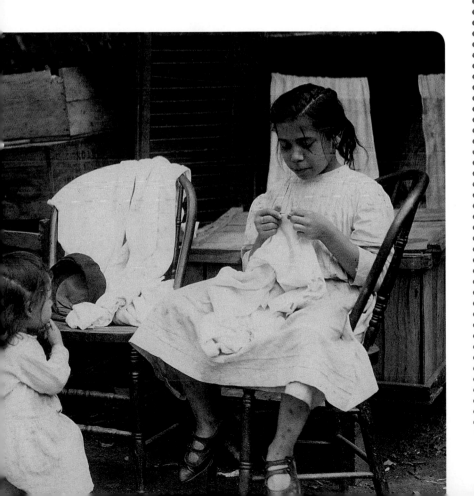

Nothing Wasted

The granny square may be one of the most widely known crochet patterns. The granny square got its start in the 1800s as a kind of early recycling. Thrifty homemakers saved their leftover bits of yarn and then used them to create multicolored squares that were sewn together. Granny squares were again popular when crochet made its comeback in the late 1960s.

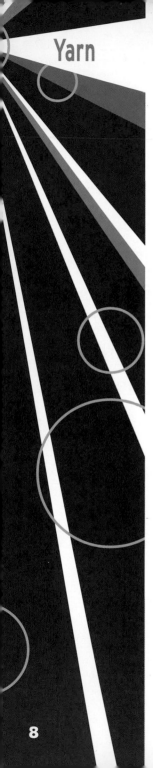

Fantastic Fibers

Are you romantic, bold, or sporty? Whatever your style, there's a yarn to match it. Yarn can be smooth or fuzzy. It can be metallic or multicolored. One important feature of any yarn is its weight, or thickness. Weight ranges from thin yarns, called fingerings, to thick, super bulky yarns. The pattern you choose will tell you what weight of yarn to buy. The yarn label lists its weight and washing

instructions. It also shows the yarn's dye lot. You should make sure the dye lot on the labels match if you are buying more than one skein, or package of yarn.

Smooth, solid, light-colored yarns are the best choice for beginners. Acrylic, man-made yarns are inexpensive and machine-washable. Yarns can be made from natural materials as well. Animal hair or fur is spun into yarns such as mohair and wool. Silk yarn comes from silkworm cocoons. Yarns also are made from plants such as bamboo and cotton.

Don't Get Tied Up in Knots!

Yarn often is sold wound into skeins. You will find it is easier to crochet if you wind your yarn into a ball before using it. Start by pulling the end of the yarn that comes from the center of the skein, not from the outside. It is much less likely to tangle that way.

Get Hooked!

You can make hundreds of items using one simple tool: the crochet hook. But a few other items may come in handy, too.

Crochet hooks: The hooked end of a crochet hook is used to make loops in your yarn. Early crochet hooks often were made from wood, bone, or the handles of spoons. Inexpensive aluminum and plastic hooks are available today. They come in many different widths. Thicker hooks are used with thicker yarns. Thinner hooks are for thinner yarns. Yarn labels often suggest the best hook size for that weight of yarn. Hooks are marked to show their size.

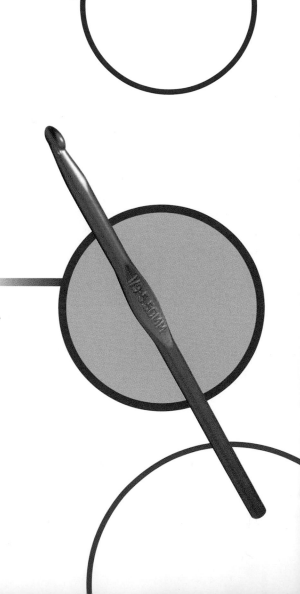

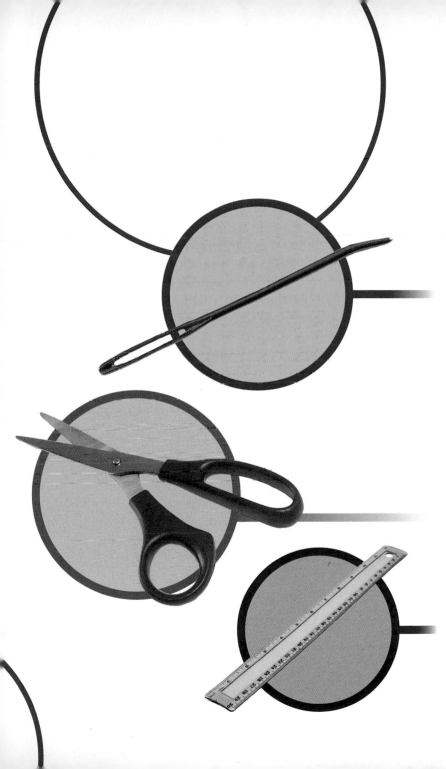

Sometimes they are marked with a letter of the alphabet. Sometimes they are marked with a number followed by the letters "mm," meaning millimeters. Some hooks have both letters and numbers. The thicker the hook, the higher the number and the further along the alphabet.

Tapestry needle: Also known as a yarn needle, a tapestry needle has a large eye that makes it easy to thread yarn through it. The needle's rounded tip makes it useful for weaving in the tails of yarn. Sometimes you will use the needle to sew together pieces of crochet.

Scissors: You will likely need scissors to cut your yarn.

Ruler: A ruler is useful when you want to measure your yarn or the size of your project.

Knot a Problem!

All crochet projects begin with a slipknot. It's easy to make once you've practiced a bit. To make a slipknot:

1. Measure a tail of yarn that is about 10 inches (25.4 centimeters) long.

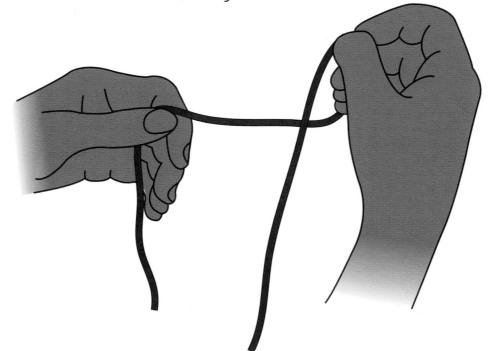

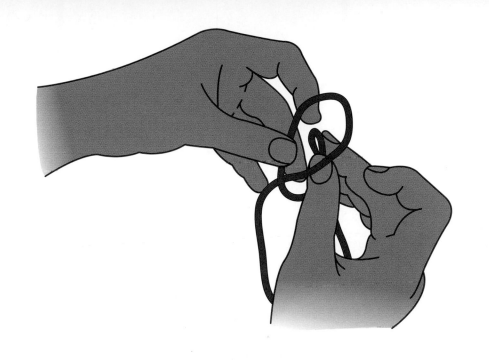

2. Make a nickel-sized loop at the 10-inch (25.4-cm) point with the working yarn, which is the yarn that comes from the ball of yarn. Where the yarn crosses to form an X, the working yarn should be on top.

3. Bring the working yarn behind and through the loop.

4. Slip the crochet hook under the new loop created by the working yarn to form a slipknot.

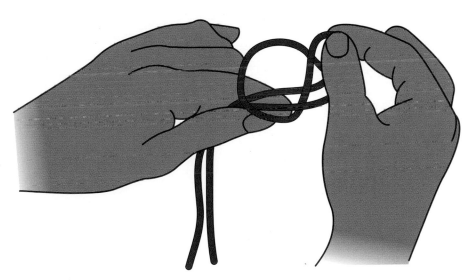

5. Draw the slipknot close to the body of the crochet hook. Don't make it really tight. The hook should still be able to slide easily inside the loop.

Hold It!

Each of your hands has a different job to do when you crochet. At first it will seem hard to get your hands to cooperate, but don't give up. Crocheting becomes easier with a little practice.

Holding your hook: There are many ways to hold the crochet hook. Different people use different holds. Some people like to hold their hooks like pencils. Some people like to hold them like knives. With practice you'll find which hold works best for you.

Holding your yarn: There are many ways to hold your yarn, too. Here's one to get you started.

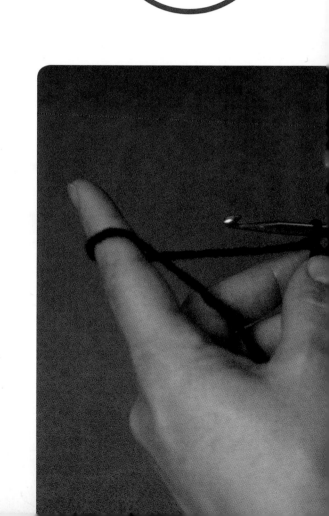

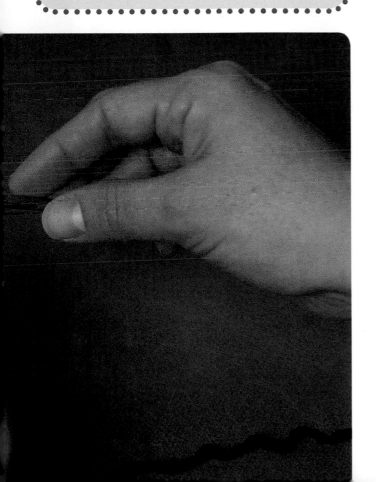

1. Pick up the hook with a slipknot on it.

2. Look at the palm of your hand that isn't holding the hook. Lay the working yarn across the pinkie, ring finger, and middle finger of that hand.

3. Fold down your pinkie and ring finger to hold the yarn in place. As you need more yarn, you will slide it under these fingers.

4. Wind the yarn under and then back over the top of your pointer finger.

5. Move your hands so that there is about 1 inch (2.5 cm) of yarn between the slipknot on the hook and the other pointer finger that is holding the yarn.

6. Reach over with the thumb and middle finger on your yarn hand. Pinch the knot on the bottom of the slipknot. The goal is to create tension in the yarn.

Making a Foundation Chain

The foundation chain is the basic building block for any crochet project. Your pattern will tell you how many stitches your chain should be. Making a chain is also a great way to practice your hook skills.

1. Begin by making a slipknot. Then, with the hook side facing you, wrap the working yarn around the hook from back to front. This is called "yarn over" in pattern directions.

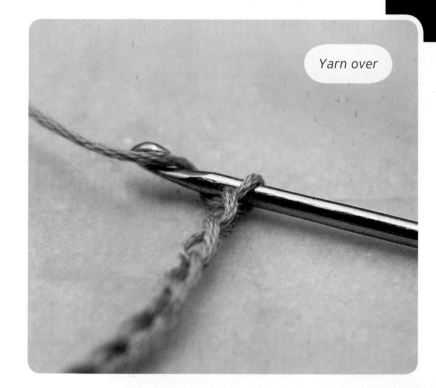

Yarn over

2. Turn the hook side away from you and pull the yarn through the loop. Pull until this new loop is close to the hook but not too tight. You have made a new chain stitch!

3. Continue to make new chain stitches. Try to keep all your stitches the same size. Make as many chain stitches as your pattern says.

You've Got It!

Are your hands tired? Take a break! With a foundation chain you can make many simple projects. You can make shoelaces, hair ties, and jewelry from foundation chains. You can braid chains together to make a belt. First decide how long you want your item to be. Then cut your working yarn, and pull it through the last loop on your hook to make a knot. Cut both tails so they are shorter.

Let the Fun Begin!

The basic crochet stitch allows you to create many fun projects.

Step 1

1. The side of your foundation chain where each stitch looks like the letter V should be facing you.

2. Count to the second stitch, or V, from the hook. The loop on the hook doesn't count as a stitch. Push the hook under the top loop of this V.

3. Wrap the working yarn over the hook from back to front. Catch the yarn with the hooked end.

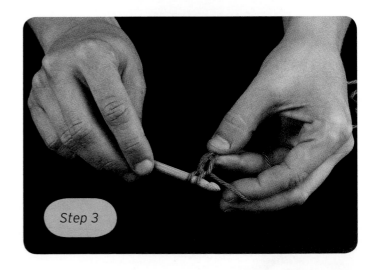

Step 3

Pull the yarn through just the chain stitch. Now you have two loops on your hook.

4. Wrap the yarn around the hook from back to front again. Pull it through both loops on your hook. You've made a single crochet stitch!

5. Insert the hook through the top loop of the next chain stitch. Make another single crochet stitch. Make a single crochet stitch in each chain stitch until you reach the end of Row 1.

6. After the last stitch, make one chain stitch on your hook. This is your turning chain. Turn your piece around to your left if you are a right-handed crocheter or to your right if you're a lefty.

7. Start Row 2 by pushing your hook through both loops on top of the first stitch. Notice that this is different from when you were working with the foundation chain.

8. Working from Step 3, continue making single crochet stitches this way until you reach the end of Row 2.

9. Make as many rows as your pattern says by following the directions for Row 2.

Step 6

Go Color Crazy!

Can't make up your mind which color is your favorite? Use more than one! Making stripes isn't nearly as hard as it looks.

1. When you reach the last stitch in a row, you will do the first half of your stitch using yarn #1. Do a single crochet stitch until the point where you have two loops on your hook.

2. This is where you will change to yarn #2. Leave a 6-inch (15.2-cm) tail of yarn #2 at the edge of your piece.

3. Wrap yarn #2 around the hook from back to front. Pull it through both stitches on your hook.

4. Continuing to use yarn #2, make your turning chain. Turn your piece around.

5. Cut off yarn #1, leaving a 6-inch (15.2-cm) tail.

6. Tie the two tails together loosely. Later you will untie and weave them into your project.

7. Continue as usual using yarn #2 until you decide to change to another color, or back to the first color.

What If You Run Out of Yarn?

Sometimes for a larger project you will need to add another ball of the same color yarn. Use the same approach as you did to add a second color for a stripe. It is easiest to add more yarn at the end of a row, so keep alert when your ball gets smaller.

Wrap It Up

The final steps you take to create a crocheted item are simple. In no time at all, you will be able to show off your latest creation!

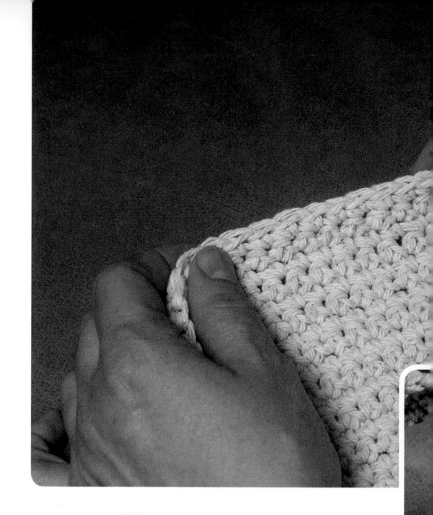

1. When you have finished the crochet stitches in your pattern, you are ready to finish your piece.

2. To make sure your stitches don't unravel, you must first fasten off your yarn.

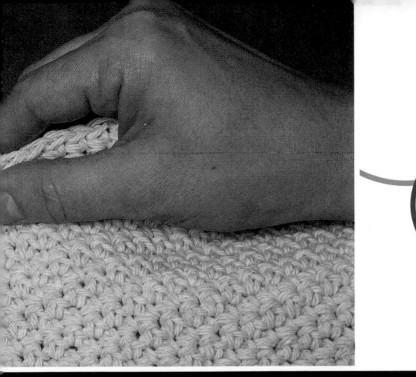

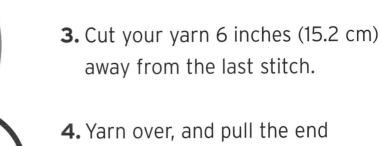

3. Cut your yarn 6 inches (15.2 cm) away from the last stitch.

4. Yarn over, and pull the end through the loop on the hook.

5. Put down your hook. Pull the tail tight until a knot forms.

6. Use a tapestry needle to weave the tails and any other yarn ends into your crocheted piece. Weave these ends in and out of 3 inches (7.6 cm) of a row of crochet.

7. Trim off any remaining ends.

Step 6

How Do You Measure Up?

Some people work their stitches tightly. Others create looser stitches. This changes the size of the finished piece. The pattern will tell you what gauge you need in order to create a certain size. The gauge is the number of stitches per inch and the number of rows per inch in your work.

Some people create stitches that are loose.

Some people like to make tighter stitches.

Try, Try Again

The yarn in your sample does not have to go to waste. It is easy to rip out crochet stitches and reuse the yarn. You also can go back and fix a mistake. Simply rip out the stitches back to the point you need to fix, and then start over. This is called frogging. Why? An old joke says it is called frogging because frogs say, "Rip it, rip it."

Before you begin a project where size matters, do a 4-inch (10.2-cm) sample to test your gauge. Use the same yarn and hook you plan to use for your project. Count how many stitches there are from top to bottom and from side to side of your test square.

Divide each number by four to get your gauge. Don't worry. If your gauge is off, you don't have to change your crochet style. Just try different size hooks until you find one that creates the right gauge.

Dishcloth

Parents, teachers, and many others agree that the most special gifts are handmade by you. Practice your crochet skills by making this simple dishcloth for one of your favorite people.

1. Chain 36 for a foundation chain.

2. Single crochet in the second chain from the hook. Single crochet in each chain to the end of the row. Chain one, and turn. You will have 35 single crochet stitches.

3. Crochet every row in single crochet stitches until your dishcloth forms a square shape.

4. Fasten off your yarn, and weave the tails into your dishcloth.

For Somebody Special

For an extra-special gift, you can make several dishcloths, each in a different color. Make an extra foundation chain in one of the colors. Using a foundation chain as a ribbon, tie your presents together with a bow for a special touch.

Striped Scarf

Show off your school colors with this striped scarf, or feature all the colors of the rainbow. Soon your friends will be asking you for one of their own!

1. Chain 21 for a foundation chain.

2. Single crochet in the second chain from the hook and in each chain across to the end of the row.

3. Crochet four rows total in yarn #1 using the single crochet stitch.

Materials

- Size G hook
- 2 or more colors of worsted weight yarn
- Tapestry needle
- Scissors

4. Crochet Row 5 up to the last stitch. Change colors as shown on pages 20-21.

5. Repeat steps 3 and 4 using yarn #2.

6. When it is time to change color again, you can switch to yarn #3 or return to yarn #1.

7. Continue making different color stripes until your scarf is the right length for you. You can test to see if it is long enough by draping it around your neck.

8. Once your scarf is the length you want, finish the fifth row of your final color.

9. Fasten off your yarn, and weave the tails into your scarf.

You Can Count on It

It is easy to accidentally add or subtract stitches when you are first learning to crochet. One way to know if you are doing this is to count your stitches every few rows. Remember, don't count the loop on the hook! You should have 20 stitches in your scarf.

Pretty Purse

You can make this pretty purse as a gift or to show off your own style. You can even make a bag to match each of your favorite outfits.

Materials

- Size G hook
- Worsted weight yarn
- Tapestry needle
- Scissors
- Ruler

1. Leave a 15-inch (38-cm) tail at the beginning of your foundation chain.

2. Chain 25 for a foundation chain.

3. Single crochet in the second chain from the hook and in each chain across. Chain one, and turn.

4. Crochet every row in single crochet stitches until your piece is 12 inches (30.5 cm) long.

5. End so that your finishing tail is diagonally across from your starting tail.

6. Fasten off your yarn leaving a 15-inch (38-cm) tail.

7. Fold your piece in half.

8. Use the tails to sew together each side of your purse. Leave the top open.

9. Weave the ends into your purse.

To make the strap:

1. Leave an 8-inch (20.3-cm) tail at the beginning of your foundation chain.

2. Make a foundation chain that is 3 feet (90 cm) long.

3. Fasten off your yarn leaving an 8-inch (20.3-cm) tail.

4. Using the tails, sew your strap securely to the purse. Weave the ends into the purse.

Afghan Section

Make these sections one at a time. Before you know it, you'll be cozy and warm under a patchwork afghan.

1. Start by checking your gauge as described on page 25. The gauge you want to achieve is nine single crochet stitches equaling 2 inches (5 cm).

2. If your test sample comes out bigger than that, try a smaller hook. If your test size comes out smaller, try a larger hook.

3. Chain 30 for your foundation chain.

4. Single crochet in the second chain from the hook and in each chain across. Chain one, and turn.

Materials

- Size G hook
- Worsted weight acrylic yarn
- Tapestry needle
- Scissors
- Ruler

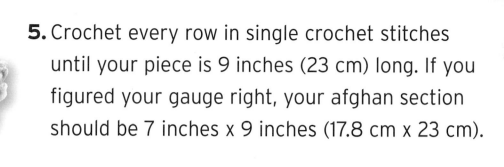

5. Crochet every row in single crochet stitches until your piece is 9 inches (23 cm) long. If you figured your gauge right, your afghan section should be 7 inches x 9 inches (17.8 cm x 23 cm).

6. Fasten off your yarn, and weave the ends into your afghan section.

7. Make another section, repeating steps 3 through 7.

8. Once you have all the sections you need (see below), it is time to connect them. Sew them together using a tapestry needle and yarn.

Putting It All Together

A full-size afghan equals 49 sections, or you can make a smaller blanket using fewer sections. A baby blanket needs just eight sections.

Lifesaver

In many countries and at different times, crochet has been more than just a fun craft. For some people, creating and selling crocheted items was an important way of making money. Even children have crocheted to help their families survive.

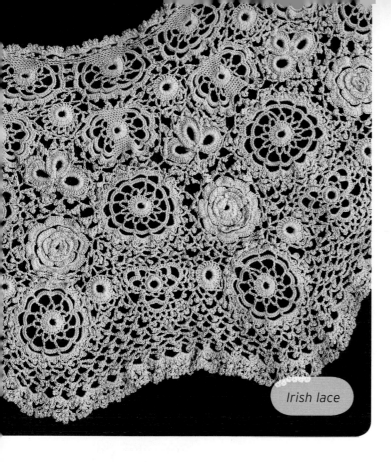
Irish lace

The most famous example of this practice was in Ireland during the potato famine of 1845 to 1850. Irish people began making a kind of crochet that looks like lace. Lace was popular at that time as a decoration for clothing and other items. However, it took a lot of time to make lace, and it was expensive. Irish crochet, as it came to be called, could be done more quickly, even though it included intricate designs such as flowers. Crochet helped many Irish families survive the famine. Some were able to earn enough money to leave Ireland for North America, and they took their crochet skills with them.

Famous Pattern Maker

Mademoiselle Riego de la Branchardière took credit for creating Irish crochet, although this is not proven. Whether she created it or not, she was important to the future of crochet. She published many pattern books between 1846 and 1887. Before then, there had been few crochet patterns that were clear and easy to follow. With her useful patterns, crochet's popularity began to grow.

Here, There, and Everywhere

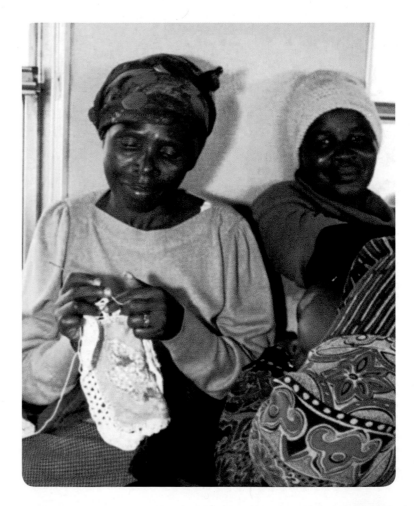

Countries all around the world have their own crochet styles and traditions. You can travel a crochet "trail" from Greece to Bosnia, from Russia to Italy, and from Sweden to Morocco. Each place will show you something interesting and unique. For example, the Mayan people of Guatemala have a long tradition of making multicolored bags using a kind of crochet called tapestry crochet.

Cute and Crocheted

A recent crochet trend had its start in Japan. Amigurumi are small, cute animals or other items. They are made from crocheting in the round.

Crochet traditions from other parts of the world can be seen in many modern cities. Kufi caps, a traditional type of African headgear, are often crocheted. People began noticing them when they became popular with the hip-hop culture. Crocheted tams, another kind of hat, help Jamaican people and others keep their dreadlocks in place. And there is a long history of crocheted yarmulkes, the skullcaps traditionally worn by Jewish men.

Crocheting for a Cause

School classes, Scout troops, and other groups of young people have found that their crochet skills can make a difference in the world. Some groups urge crafters to make and donate caps for cancer patients.

A group called Warm Up America! has donated thousands of afghans to those in need. It all began when a woman named Evie Rosen of Wausau, Wisconsin, decided she wanted to help the homeless. She asked everyone she knew to knit or crochet 7-inch x 9-inch (17.8-cm x 23-cm) sections that could be joined together. By 1995, word of the project spread. Since then people from all across the United States have pitched in to help.

Warm Up America! sections

You can create a Warm Up team in your community. Ask your friends and family to join you in making sections. You can plan regular meetings so your team members can crochet together. Once you have 49 sections, sew them together. You can donate the afghan to a hospital or shelter in or near your hometown.

Crochet Sets Trends

In recent years crochet has played a starring role on high-fashion runways. Big-name designers such as Marc Jacobs and Roberto Cavalli have presented fashion lines that featured crocheted clothing and accessories. Crochet has turned up in the form of bikinis, sandals, shawls, purses, and dresses. The clothes that go on sale in stores mimic these runway fashions.

Celebrities have helped to make crocheted clothing popular. On her TV show, Jessica Simpson wore a crocheted

Fancy That!

Some designers use crochet to make fancy jewelry.

Martha Stewart wears her crocheted poncho.

shawl by designer Cecilia De Bucourt. In 2005, Martha Stewart wore a crocheted poncho created by a prison inmate. Both fashions started a flurry of interest in crochet. Women wanted to buy shawls and ponchos just like the items they saw on TV. Crafters hunted for patterns so they could make the items for themselves.

What Happened When?

| 1800 | 1820 | 1840 | 1860 | 1880 |

1846-1887 Riego de la Branchardière publishes many books that include crochet patterns.

1824 The women's magazine *Pénelopé*, published in Holland, begins printing crochet patterns.

1880 American artist Mary Cassatt paints her sister in the picture *Lydia Crocheting in the Garden at Marly*.

1812 Scottish "shepherd's knitting," a simple crochet stitch, is described in a book.

1845-1850s Crochet provides income for Irish families that otherwise might have starved during the potato famine.

1890 **1950** **1970** **2000** **2005** **2010**

Late 1880s Crochet is banned from needlecraft classes in Prussian schools because, unlike sewing and knitting, it is not considered useful.

2008 In February, more than 50,000 people attended Knit-Out & Crochet at the Mall of America in Bloomington, Minnesota. The event included many activities, such as free lessons and fashion shows.

2004 A survey by the Craft Yarn Council of America shows that 53 million Americans know how to knit or crochet.

1970s Crocheted items such as granny squares grow in popularity across North America.

1950 DuPont begins producing acrylic fiber; the growing availability of less-expensive synthetics such as acrylic has a major impact on yarn choices.

2005 The Lycos Internet site lists crochet as the No. 10 top fad.

43

Fun Crocheting Facts

Lisa Gentry set the record as the fastest crocheter in 2005. She crocheted 170 stitches per minute!

In 1997, a Cornell University professor named Daina Taimina realized that she could use crochet to create a model portraying a unique kind of geometry. Now other mathematicians also are using crochet.

When Boise State University star Ian Johnson makes headlines, it's not always for his amazing football skills. His crochet skills have grabbed the attention of the media and YouTube.

Famous children's book author Laura Ingalls Wilder was one of many American pioneer women who crocheted.

There are hundreds of crochet stitches and stitch combinations. Some have unusual names, such as checkerboard, broomstick, and pineapple. When you are ready, you can find a book or search the Internet to learn some of these stitches and stitch combinations.

Crocheting Words to Know

acrylic: type of yarn

amigurumi: Japanese-inspired crochet trend for creating animal figures

crocheting in the round: crochet patterns that circle around a center rather than going in straight rows

dye lot: balls or skeins of yarn to which the same coloring has been added at the same time

fasten off: finish a crochet piece by securing the end tail

foundation chain: basic series of chain stitches that a crocheted piece is built on

frogging: ripping out crochet stitches

gauge: number of stitches per inch and the number of rows per inch in your work

granny square: popular crochet pattern that uses scrap yarn

shepherd's knitting: old form of crochet with roots in colder European countries

skein: loose, thick coil of yarn

tail: end of the yarn that gives you something to hold as you begin to crochet and shows you where you started

tapestry crochet: crochet that uses multiple colors of yarn and creates the appearance of a woven piece

tapestry needle: needle with a large eye and a blunt tip; also known as a yarn needle

turning chain: extra chain stitch made at the end of a row to turn the stitch

weight: thickness of yarn

working yarn: yarn that leads off of the ball of yarn

worsted: medium weight yarn

Other Words to Know

afghan: large blanket

dreadlocks: hairstyle in which the hair is grown long and worn in thick, ropelike strands

intricate: detailed and complicated

kufi caps: traditional African headgear, often worn by Muslim men

vice versa: Latin phrase that means "the other way around"

Where to Learn More

MORE BOOKS TO READ

Davis, Jane. *Crochet: Fantastic Jewelry, Hats, Purses, Pillows & More*. New York: Lark Books, 2005.

Haab, Sherri, and Michelle Haab. *Way to Crochet: Cool, Easy Projects for Kids of All Ages*. New York: Watson-Guptill Publications, 2008.

Holetz, Julie Armstong. *Crochet Away!* New York: Price Stern Sloan, 2006.

ON THE ROAD

World Famous Crochet Museum
61855 Highway 62
Joshua Tree, CA 92252

American Folk Art Museum
45 W. 53rd St.
New York, NY 10019
212/265-1040

ON THE WEB

For more information on this topic, use FactHound.

1. Go to *www.facthound.com*
2. Type in this book ID: 0756538610
3. Click on the *Fetch It* button.

FactHound will find the best Web sites for you.

INDEX

ABOUT THE AUTHOR

Lisa Bullard is the author of more than 40 books for young readers. She has enjoyed doing many different handcrafts since she was a little girl. When she crochets, her two cats chase the ball of yarn around her living room. Bullard lives in Minneapolis, Minnesota, where her family depends on her to make scarves to keep them warm during the winter months.